Introduction 5

The Three Goals 6

Visualize and Materialize 11

Action = Results 13

Maintaining the Quality of Meetings 16

Adapt-Improvise-Overcome 19

Saving Time 22

Developing Meeting Skills 22

Preparing for a Meeting 27

What If We Don't Have Meetings? 30

Conclusion 31

Introduction

To have meetings or not to have meetings? That is the $64,000,000 question. Why *do* we have meetings? What difference do they make? Do we really understand the value of meetings? Too many times we excuse ourselves from meetings, and we also excuse others. "OK, I understand you can't invite the people. Yes, I know you can't prepare all the material. Of course, I understand you can't be there." But let's ask this question: What if you could? What if you could invite the people? What if you could attend? What sort of difference would it make in your business? How would having meetings change your lifestyle? How could they change your children's future? It is definitely something to think about. Let's consider the possibilities.

Oh, the Possibilities

To introduce the value of meetings, I am going to share a true story. A couple of years ago I had a meeting in Hope, New Jersey, where only three people showed up. There were seats for 80 to 100 people and only *three* people showed up. We could have just gone home, but I went ahead and did a slide presentation like there were 150 or 200 people in the room. The three people present kept turning around, looking to the back of the room to see if there really were any more people there. I was just really going after it, getting excited and sharing all kinds of examples with them, really going the extra mile to get them to understand what the products could do, the real power of the products. I talked about the power of the marketing plan, and the amazing power that comes from sharing with people. I also focused on the power that results because we are involved in an industry that really makes a difference. (That is one of the absolute exciting things that we have to do—share the value of what we do with others.)

And you know what happened? As a result of that meeting, I have one of my top sales leaders. She has created a huge organization with tremendous volume and is immensely successful—and she was one of those three people sitting there. Now go back to the questions I asked at the beginning. How have meetings changed this woman's life? How has attending meetings affected her future? It's amazing! It just shows how consistency, persistence and looking at the big picture (even when you're working small) really mean something.

THE THREE GOALS

There are three main things we want to try to accomplish with meetings in this business. Number one: EDUCATE. Number two: EMPOWER. Number three: INCREASE AWARENESS AND VISION. These three parts work together as a whole to help us understand what it is we can do now and what it is we have the potential to do. I think that our minds and spirits expand as our visualization and realization expand. And meetings are there to help us visualize and realize what can be done. They serve as reminders of what we should be doing and what is possible.

EDUCATE

Meetings are for the message. One of the basic reasons to have meetings is to educate people so that they understand the message. This can be the message of the life-changing ability of the products or it can be the message of the life-changing ability of the marketing plan. People will understand the message of empowerment, they'll realize the independence they can create from this, they'll be reminded about the lifestyle they can get, and they'll remember that this is a real deal.

A wonderful example of sharing the message comes from Linda, a young lady in my downline who was running last summer and slipped and fell, shattering three or four of her back vertebrae. She was in an upper body cast, had to use a cane and could barely get around. She experienced tremendous pain, but with time she slowly improved, little by little.

She was able to attend a meeting we had a few weeks ago where we introduced a new product and talked about the three major things it is really good for—arthritis, diabetes, and pain. There really aren't a lot of herbs that combat serious pain, so at the meeting we all got really excited about this product that can be effective in that area. Well, Linda listened and learned. Then she went home and found some capsules of the new product that she had recently ordered. She took them through the course of the next day and the following morning, when she woke up, she was amazed to find that she could get out of bed without pain. She didn't have pain in her neck, she didn't have pain in her back, and she was able to get up and move around. She continued taking the product for a few more days and continued to improve. When she came to our next meeting, she was able to stand up and give her testimony without using her cane. And let me tell you something, she lit everybody up! We were all so excited—what a meeting that was.

SHARE THE MESSAGE

There was a fellow at that same meeting, Jim, who went home inspired and decided he was going to use the same product. He took it twice a day and made a tea out of it. He could not believe the change that resulted. He is now able to walk to places he hasn't been able to to walk for ten years. The pain in his legs is non-existent, and he just can't believe it. An 83-year-old friend of his is also taking the product and is driving her daughter nuts because instead of sitting in a chair all day, she's running up and down the stairs, bothering her daughter and always trying to find out what everybody else is doing.

So why do I relate these stories? Simply to show the value of meetings for sharing the message. The sharing that took place at one meeting made Linda aware of the value of a new product.

At the second meeting she shared her testimony of the tremendous results possible from using that product. Jim attended both those meetings, so he decided to use the product too. He had his success and shared it with everyone at the next meeting. And now we've had three meetings that have been absolutely awesome.

This gives you an idea of the type of energy and vitality that can come out of meetings, one after another after another. The growth we've had with this one product has been massive in a short period of time. You begin to see how things start to move when meetings share the message and really get things going.

EMPOWER

As we become educated about our business and our products, we also become empowered. And the things we learn at meetings raise our level of confidence not only in the products and the business, but our level of trust in each other is increased. At meetings we teach each other, listen to each other. Think how exciting it is to watch another person learn and progress—to see the new people change from timid beginners to powerful sales leaders. With information, confidence and responsibility, they become empowered.

One simple thing people need to realize is that they will be most successful when they work to help empower their group. People have to start seriously looking beyond themselves if they want to develop a huge organization. I look at how something can help thousands of people in my downline, not just how it can help me. We really have to have people ask the question, "Will this help empower my group? And if it does, when do I need to get this information to them? As soon as possible." This is extremely critical. Let me share a story to illustrate my point.

A few months ago I had a meeting which a really mixed group of people attended. Several of the people were from organizations that aren't a part of mine, but I open my meetings to them and I transfer information and educate them. It is interesting, though, that it took them some time to learn to do the same. The weekend before our meeting, these individuals attended an education seminar and never told anybody else about it. They assumed we knew about it, and we didn't. It was very interesting how they simply assumed. I went to our meeting with material to hand out that I had written by hand. I wrote and cut and pasted things together to make sure everyone had the information because I thought it was that critical. But these people had already received the information over the weekend and had other handouts already. Yet they hadn't shared the information!

WILL THIS EMPOWER MY GROUP?

This story clearly shows the difference between the person who simply thinks about what's good for him or herself, and the person who is trying to empower the group. Dynamic sales leaders are constantly looking for ways to increase their personal development and then they share what they learn in order to empower their group. The beauty of it is that by empowering the group, they are also empowering themselves.

Increase Awareness and Vision

As we become educated and empowered, our level of awareness will itself increase. If we are aware of the potential we have for success, nothing will stop us. And our awareness ties in completely with our vision. There are multiple types of vision. For example, in a recent meeting we discussed the fact that a lot of people are challenged simply by the fact that they have very narrow vision. Tunnel vision is what happens when you only allow yourself to look through a small pipe, say six or seven inches in diameter, and that's your total vision. Instead of looking 180 degrees around you and using your peripheral vision, you're only seeing a small part of what's out there. How can you be aware of opportunities for growth and change if your vision is so restricted? You simply see a limited amount!

Even worse is when your vision becomes so narrow that it can be called funnel vision. People with this kind of vision act like they have a funnel on their head—the large part is on their face letting them look through what reduces down to a very narrow hole. What sort of long-range view can you have from the inside of a funnel? For whatever reason, they actually choose to reduce their vision and so approach life with a serious handicap. And too many people tend to be very "funnel vision-ish." When it comes to their health, finances, attitudes or abilities, their vision is very narrow, very cut-down as compared to what it could be. They are so narrowed that their chances of being able to change anything to any large degree are practically nonexistent.

We really have to work to avoid this tendency to reduce our vision, and that's why we have meetings—to try and help expand vision and to empower. Part of expanding our business vision is to expand in all ways—physically, mentally, spiritually, etc. We all need to work at expanding our whole vision because what happens is that we get into a comfort zone, a place where things seem easy and we would like to stay. We start to resist change, and that is our vision begins to narrow. Another common thing that happens is that our daily lives become routine and ordinary. In a lot of ways we are beaten into conformity. Our dreams and aspirations get neutralized, and we are consumed by the effort needed just to complete the day. The result is that we get caught up living for the weekends, focusing on momentary pleasures and completely casting off or putting aside our dreams, goals and aspirations. We lose our long-range vision, and that can be very detrimental.

CATCH THE VISION

So, once again, the value of meetings becomes obvious. Meetings help us continue to catch the vision of our business. For positive change to occur in our lives, we need to stimulate vision. We need to look ahead. We don't walk with our heads down, looking at our feet. We walk with our heads up and our feet just naturally go. We need to use our minds more, make plans more, not worry every two seconds about what's going on right here. We have to understand and we have to believe that we're moving in the right direction and that we will eventually get the right results—the results we want.

VISUALIZE AND MATERIALIZE

Visualization is an amazing concept. Like Mark Victor Hansen says, we need to visualize before we can materialize. In other words, we need to mentally "see" ourselves doing something so that we can push ourselves to expand and grow. As a small example, let me tell you about a meeting I had on Wednesday night. We talked about going out and getting the Rob Report, a magazine that reports on the rich and the famous. It tells about their cars, planes, yachts, land, jewelry, and recreation as well as their concepts, ideas and businesses. It's an awesome report because it's tremendously mind expanding. And the whole point of the meeting was to help us realize that what we need to do is visualize ourselves in the places we want to be, visualize ourselves as successful, and then get things moving in the right direction.

Right now, we live in the most progressive time in the history of the world. We are able to massively increase our standard of living, to enjoy tremendous amenities and technologies. We just need to visualize the possibilities and ask, "Why not? Why not me? Why can't I have a better, bigger income? Why can't I be more successful?" The world is out there and there is so much to be done. There are so many people to be empowered. There is so much to be learned and shared and put together, it's incredible!

DREAM BOARDS

We all need to start really employing vision. One of the ways to do that is with what I call a dream board. Basically, a dream board is a bulletin board, a poster board, or a place on the wall in your office or home where you can put things to remind yourself of what you want to accomplish. You use this board to plan the size of your business, its expansion, and your position within it. On this board you plan your trips, outline your income goals, list the degrees you want to earn. Put pictures on your dream board of places you want to be, things you want to make a part of your life. Try and update it continually with your new dreams, wishes and goals—a dream board is not a stagnant thing. We are dynamic, we change constantly, and our dream board should reflect that.

The reason a dream board is so important is because it feeds our subconscious mind on a continual basis. Of course, after awhile, we don't even see it—we don't see it consciously, that is. But we recognize it subconsciously, which is even more important. Our subconscious makes up 80 percent of our brain so when we feed it with everything we have mounted on our dream board, we're empowering 80 percent of our brain. We have to realize that our dream boards are the visualization of our goals, and when we display them, they enter our subconscious.

I often think of the scientists who were trying to figure out why someone who was a certified genius would not be getting ahead and yet another person who was supposedly "average" was doing absolutely spectacular things. One of the things they found out is that the "average" person did not use their subconscious mind just to record history or remember facts and figures. Instead they used their subconscious mind to project into the future and think about, "If I could do this, how would I do it?" or "There must be a way to do it—let me think about it and figure out the way." It is a way of life for them. People who learn to use their subconscious in this way empower themselves tremendously. It pays to dream!

ACTION = RESULTS

I have all kinds of people in network marketing tell me that they're not getting enough results. I say if you want massive results, you've got to take massive action. Meetings are just one of the things you can do to create massive action—meetings, newsletters, cassette tapes, plugging people into video programs your company has, etc. People ask how many meetings do you need? If you're doing a massive number of meetings I can guarantee you're getting massive results. That's the equation. How you deal with the equation is up to you.

KEEP THE MOMENTUM GOING

I happen to like weekly meetings. A lot of people like a monthly meeting, but I feel there are too many things happening in this industry. The industry is moving extremely fast—we're in a major boom era. The next ten, fifteen, twenty years are going to be outstanding. And I think the people that don't have weekly meetings, people that only have meetings once a month, are going to see the need for change. Change happens— and we need to be on top of any changes.

WE NEED TO BE ON TOP OF CHANGE

A good example would be if the price of the distributor kit changes from $39.95 to $19.95. As soon as I hear that, I'm able to announce it at the weekly meeting and get the momentum immediately going. The fact that a person can come in and receive a distributor kit for half the cost is great—obviously the number $19.95 works a lot better than the number $39.95. And it's the idea that I'm able to get this information to my group right away that is very, very important. If I'm having weekly meetings I don't have to wait until next month to announce the change and my group is that far ahead.

Obviously, I'll also try to get the information out by talking to different people and doing different things. But with a meeting I can already get my distributors and my sales leaders on track.

Let me plug the value of weekly meetings with one more example. Let's say that the company you're with announces a mid-month special: From now until the end of the month, if you buy three of a certain product you will get another one free. Along with that, if you buy four of a second product, you will get another free item. And let's say the company has thirty items involved in this special offer which will end on the last day of the month. This could be a super win situation for distributors and sales leaders because of the volume. It is also a great situation for the company because of the opportunity to get the product into more people's hands and the surge in the use of the product. It could be a positive thing for everyone involved.

But, if I had had my monthly meeting before the special was announced, I would have missed the opportunity to inform my people and help everyone see the value and the big perspective of such opportunities. And I would also have to do a lot of calling and talking to make sure than most of my group knew about the special before it ended! With a weekly meeting, on the other hand, I would be able to announce the special as soon as I knew about it and everyone in attendance would benefit. With weekly meetings we almost have the minuteman effect—the idea that we can react to things very quickly, via the meeting and the information available there. With weekly meetings we can take advantage of any new information or change, and that allows us to get up to speed more quickly. What momentum!

WITH WEEKLY MEETINGS, WE HAVE THE MINUTEMAN EFFECT. . .

Another plus for having weekly meetings is that it is easier to miss a meeting and still keep things going, If you have monthly meetings, what do you do if something comes up? What if the weather blows the meeting out, or what if the meeting falls on a night that is a holiday and you get a low attendance? Simply said, you've lost momentum. By missing just a few monthly meetings you can easily lose two, three, four months momentum and that costs you severely.

Attitude and Attendance

What do you do when somebody says, "I'd like to do an herbal hour at my house Thursday afternoon," and you already have a meeting scheduled for Thursday night somewhere else? You have to choose whether to attend afternoon *and* night or afternoon *or* night. Ideally, your response should not be one or the other—it should be the meeting at night *and* the meeting in the afternoon. Some days you're going to double up and triple up, but, if you're doing it correctly, you're doubling and tripling your results—which is absolutely super.

Stay On Track

Another reason to have weekly meetings came up today in a conversation I had with Debbie, Doug, and Larry. We were discussing the fact that we constantly need to be working with our minds and keeping our minds positive and going forward. We need to know what we're doing and what we're not doing. We need to know if the newsletters are getting out, if the information is available, whether or not we have momentum going, whether or not there's activity, whether or not people are using, fielding and sharing the products. It's all very important. The challenge is that sometimes a little doubt slips in. We ask ourselves, "Am I doing enough today? Am I doing this? Am I doing that?" We start to doubt our abilities. But you know what? That's natural. Everything has a natural propensity to go off course with time and we just have to fight it. One of the wonderful things about meetings is that they help to keep us on track.

MAINTAINING THE QUALITY OF MEETINGS

After all this talk about the importance and value of meetings, I need to address the need of keeping meetings worthwhile. There are times when information on new products is flowing and things are really moving and people feel that the time they spend in meetings is time well spent. But there are other times when, for whatever reason, things seem to slow down and the the information flow gets very flat. In other words, there is basically nothing new coming from the company during a particular month or at a particular time. People in the field get the feeling that there is just nothing going on.

Really, however, there are always things going on, even if it's not obvious. New and different products are being analyzed and researched, different ways of obtaining things are being explored, new bottles and containers are being looked into, along with various other things. There is always something going on in the company, but the distributorship and sales leaders may not be aware of it so they feel that things have just gone flat. How does this sort of mood affect our meetings? How can we maintain momentum when we move into a lull period, waiting for the company to output the results of their study and research?

This is the time when we use meetings to work on personal development. We have meetings on leadership skills, listening skills, goal making and planning, and whatever other personal qualities people feel they need to work on. In this way, we keep the momentum going and probably even increase it.

We have to always work to keep enthusiasm levels high, and the only way we can do it is through cassette tapes, conference calls, and meetings. These are the ways that we are stimulated, focused, and kept on track. The ultimate gain from any meeting is momentum. People get excited again about their goals and dreams, and they get some momentum going in their personal lives. The leaders who do the meetings are able to keep up with the dreams, goals, and aspirations of the business, and they're reminded of all the things that they want to do. Like I said before, meetings keep everyone on track. You're able to fight the propensity to get off track with meetings, and you're able to empower yourself and keep your awareness level up.

Energy and Information

Meetings are the glue that keeps us all together and allows us to constantly be disseminating information, ideas, and strategies to be able to do different things. As far as I'm concerned, a meeting can be like the sun—the center of the solar system—to give us all the energy and ideas we need to call and talk to people and work in the best way. Meetings become the catalyst. They impel you to get out there and do everything else you need to be doing.

MEETINGS—THE GLUE THAT HOLDS US TOGETHER

Meetings generate energy and learning. Let's say we have twenty or thirty people coming to a Tuesday night meeting. We bring up a new subject, discuss a new product, get quite excited about it. On Wednesday somebody finds an article about the product, makes note of it and photocopies it, and then comes back to the Thursday morning meeting and shares the new information with the group. Now twenty people are working as resource centers, getting information, passing it back and forth, helping each other learn. And it's amazing what happens. The synergy grows and everyone benefits. Momentum begins to massively multiply.

The energy and renewed vitality we get from meetings expresses itself in various ways. It can be through financial gain, increased self-confidence, or simply an improved state of health. A woman who came to our meeting today has had a problem with bone density loss—five percent a year for the last five years. A twenty-five percent bone-density loss. The wonderful thing is that, after attending meetings and gaining the incentive to research her condition, she's actually beginning to see, feel, and understand what she's doing. She's starting to understand calcium, calcium absorption, and bone density much better. She's starting to understand the things she can do to change and move this whole thing in a more positive direction. She is more confident, more happy, and her vision is clearer. Meetings do give us life and energy!

Feedback and Learning

When I give a meeting, I learn just as much, if not more, than the people who come. The reason is that I get good feedback from people, from their excitement. I may share something with them about which I'm extremely passionate and enthused, and they may think it's no big deal. It's kind of interesting to see how they respond. I've had other times that I didn't think something was a big deal and then everybody else got all excited about it. So, it's interesting to get the feedback from people.

Another important thing to remember is that in this business we have people at all levels. New people are constantly coming in and we address them and have information for them. We also need information for the intermediate and advanced people. What I try to do is obviously mix it all so that everyone walks away with more than enough from a meeting. And they learn from each other! It's tremendously exciting to watch the sharing and the energy that happen during a good meeting.

Learn From the Newbies

At any meeting you get a good mix of sales leaders/distributors and new people. That's one of the things I think is excellent about meetings—the fact that you are constantly having new people come and having that feeling of newness in your meetings. One of the challenges with not having meetings is ıat you start to get a little bit removed from new people. And ew people are your life-line, your whole growth factor. I call ıem Newbies. I get excited about Newbies because they ask uestions that put you back to square one. You'd better remem-er square one if you plan to get anywhere. You'd better know our marketing plan and your products. And with the Newbies ɔ keep you on your toes, you will. And everyone prospers.

ƆRUSH THE LEARNING CURVE

I think one of the biggest key reasons for meetings is to crush the learning curve. With weekly meetings, if they're really going after it, everyone will be able to learn in a month or two what it took people like me three or five years to learn. I have people who come to my meetings and double up—they come on Tuesday night, Thursday mornings, and when we sometimes have Wednesday night training meetings, they come to those too. We really get things moving and then those people can go do the same for their groups. You always need to pass on what you learn!

ADAPT-IMPROVISE-OVERCOME

One of my favorite concepts is the idea of "adapt-improvise-overcome." In other words, you've got to adapt to the environment you're in, especially when you're doing meetings. A meeting is a very intense environment because people want a lot of information. That's one of the reasons it's crucial to have background. You need to have attended all kinds of classes and seminars, read books, and listened to tapes so that you're informed and up-to-date. That way you can adapt to the audience and answer all questions. And if you don't have the answer, you know where to go to find it.

Improvising and overcoming are big parts of every meeting. For example, occasionally there's going to be somebody who feels like they were dragged to the meeting and they're going to have an attitude. What I try to do is ask them what questions they have and if they say nothing and want nothing, I just let them be. Let it be their own experience. Do the best you can.

Besides the people who have an occasional attitude, sometimes someone else will not let the meeting progress. Let's say you're holding a meeting, an herbal hour, and someone in the audience is quite outspoken and continually asking questions about asthma. You need to veer from your planned topic a bit and address that particular topic, help that person understand things that are good for asthma and spend some time on the issue. Be sure and go back to the group and ask if there are other suggestions or questions. That way you've accomplished something and the meeting can continue as you planned.

If that same person continues to consume the whole meeting then what you need to do then is overcome the situation by starting to ask questions of other individuals in attendance. "Do you know anybody that has arthritis?" "Do you know anybody that has diabetes?" "Do you know anybody that has heart disease?" By using different lead questions or any particular personal questions that you have, you can move into other areas and allow other people to participate. By adapting things slightly you can change the whole course of the meeting.

Another important part of the "adapt-improvise-overcome" scenario is dealing with objections and doubts. For example, in one of your weekly meetings you decide to spend some time explaining and discussing the network marketing plan. What do you do if somebody in the group speaks up and says "Is this one of those pyramid schemes?" Obviously you need to be able to address the question and overcome that objection. Don't just answer "No" and move on. You need to acknowledge the validity of the question with something like, "It's good you brought that up because it's something a lot of people wonder about." Ask for feedback from the group. You can discuss the fact that in 1979 the FTC declared network marketing to be a legitimate business. Then focus on the best parts of the business and drive home that one of the best ways to market anything is to distribute through networking. After that sort of discussion, people will feel satisfied and confident.

As a final example of how important it is to adapt, improvise and overcome, let me share a personal experience.There was a time when I went to do meetings with a projector and a screen. One particular night I went to an area where there had been a severe thunder and lightning storm. It knocked out all the electricity in the whole area so we were going to call the meeting off. But, because it was a neighborhood meeting, everybody still wanted to come. They had all kinds of questions they wanted to ask and have answered. So, amazingly enough, we actually had the meeting using only candles for light. I thought the meeting would last about an hour or so, but it ended up lasting about three and a half hours. What a great example of adapting, improvising and overcoming!

A lot of times when you do a meeting, you may be prepared in one particular area, and that is fine. Just remember that you need to be flexible enough to be able to bend and move with the group. What is important is that their questions get answered, not yours. People love having their questions answered. They love to come back with more questions that they feel confident will get answered.

PEOPLE LOVE HAVING THEIR QUESTIONS ANSWERED

One of the reasons I find someone constantly trying to be the sole person asking questions at a meeting is because they've never been to a meeting where they've had their questions answered. I get them to calm down, and realize that I am going to be there, I will help them, I am not going to run away, I will be back. So they start to relax and realize that they will get their questions answered and that they will find sources to help them get answers to other questions. Then they will learn that they too can adapt, improvise and overcome.

SAVING TIME

One of the reasons for having at least one meeting a week is that in network marketing there are a lot of people telephoning each other. After awhile you can have your people, your customers, your distributors calling you on a constant basis, every two minutes about every little thing. And that can take up a lot of time. It's not that we don't want to answer their questions, it's just that many people want an answer whenever questions happen to pop into their heads, and they have no discipline to write them down or get them in some sort of order and present them at a meeting. That's the purpose of the meeting! It's also about training and educating people to understand what's going on.

A MEETING IS A TREMENDOUS TIME-SAVER

So, when people call up and have questions, you can say, "You know what? We'll cover this at Tuesday night's meeting." or "This is a great topic! Let me do this—instead of spending twenty minutes on the phone with you to explain this, I need to have you there at the meeting to make sure you ask this question so I can cover it with the whole group. The whole group needs to know this stuff!" When people ask questions, be they customers or distributors, you funnel them into the meeting. And if they say they can't make it, then you let them know that when they can, you'll be there.

The meeting eventually becomes a tremendous time-saver because it allows you to do your work throughout the day. You can work on prospecting, newsletters, sending out cassette tapes, talking about videos, lining up the next meeting, figuring out what the sales are, ordering products, or reading a book that has to do with the business—be it a DHEA book, a book on leadership or a book about developing yourself, your life force, your energy. Whatever you do is terrific, because what you do, you can teach others to do. And that's important. One of our most valuable assets is our time and we need to learn to maximize every moment we have.

Ask Questions

At the end of the meeting, I invariably have five or six people rush up to me with questions they think are personal. Not so! Almost all questions are important and can be asked in front of the group. In fact, 90 to 99 percent of the questions I'm asked after a meeting should have been asked at the meeting to empower the whole group. Not only that, but a lot of times the people who ask the questions after the meetings don't really do much with the answer. If the same question is asked in front of the group, chances are you'll have someone else in the group who is going to do something with the answer. Somebody is going to take the answer and put it into action.

Secret Agents

Meetings have to be long enough that you're able to cover enough material, but short enough that people want to come back to the next meeting. And they should come back excited and wanting more. Meetings should catapult people into action. You don't want people to just come to a meeting and then do nothing but wait until next week's meeting. You want to challenge the people to share. Ron Booker, a good friend of mine in the business, teaches that we don't want to be "secret agents." Too many people have become secret agents in that they don't tell anybody about the products that could help them, they don't say anything about opportunities that are open to them, they don't operate like this is a personal business that they can work themselves and grow with. We need to learn to talk and share and realize that we grow as the people around us grow.

TALK ABOUT THE PRODUCTS

One thing you want to do at meetings is continue to cover basic products and introduce any new ones. You want to be able to teach about their benefits and advantages. Meetings allow us to be able to get feedback from people, and they spur us to action—create energy. All of a sudden you're making handouts, flyers and newsletters to relate the information that comes about from the meetings. Meetings can become tremendous masterminding experiences and tremendous energy forces in building our business.

DEVELOPING MEETING SKILLS

Let's say you have a sales leader in your area that's doing meetings, and perhaps doing them on a weekly basis. It may be wise for you to plug into those meetings. But you do not want to become mesmerized, fantasized and hypnotized by the fact that that person is constantly doing a meeting. You still need to develop the skills necessary to have a good meeting. You need to start having meetings, if not once a month, maybe twice a month. You need to have meetings so you get more of a feel for meetings. You start to become more relaxed with them and let them work for you, as opposed to beating yourself up mentally because you feel unprepared or under confident. Don't approach a meeting as if it's a big awesome undertaking. It's not. It's a very basic thing and it's sort of like exercise—the more you do it the easier and more rewarding it gets.

There is a definite difference between *going* to a meeting and *doing* a meeting. The level of responsibility is very different, as is your total response to the meeting. You get out of a "judgement" mode and get into a "doing" mode. It's good for your success rate!

To do a good meeting you simply need to be tuned it to what your people want and you need to be creative. Let me share an easy idea with you on how to do a meeting. I call it "meeting in a box." It's a very simple idea, but one that works every time I use it. What I do is take a shipping box from one of the companies that sends me bulk products and before I go to the meeting I put in a series of different products, maybe ten, fifteen or even twenty products. At the meeting I explain that I'm going to show everyone how to do an effective, simple meeting. This is for the people who think they can't put a meeting together—they need to know that they can do just as well as anyone. And what we do is just start pulling out each product and talking about it. We discuss what it is, what it's good for. Some people share information about it and others give testimonials about it. Everybody gets involved and this simple kind of meeting stimulates the entire group and we have fun.

MEETING IN A BOX

THE PRACTICAL SIDE OF MEETINGS

SIZE OF MEETINGS

How many people have to be at a meeting? I'm a firm believer that it's not the number of people—it's the quality of people. If you have a meeting with only two or three people, but they are people who are serious and interested, that's enough. You just start building with them and you start to work on direction and goals. As time goes on, attendance will go up and your numbers will go up. But don't let numbers discourage you. They can be quite deceiving because they don't show the attitude and the learning and the excitement of the people who do attend the meeting. A meeting with three of your best people is always better than a meeting with fifteen people who don't give a rip and will waste your time.

CONSISTENCY AND STABILITY

If you're going to have meetings, what you want to do is determine that meetings will be held every second and fourth Tuesday, or every Tuesday night, or the first Wednesday of the month. Whatever schedule you can handle, keep it going. Be consistent. You might have to change the time or the day you have a meeting, but you keep the magic of the meeting going. Regardless of what goes on, you are there! I've learned that I can't cancel my meetings. I have hundreds of people that could possibly be coming to the meeting and there is no way I could call everybody. Basically, I show up or I have somebody else show up, regardless of what else is going on. Even if it's a blizzard I go over to the meeting place because if somebody shows up, at least I tell them we'll meet for a few minutes, answer a couple of questions, and go on from there. The thing to remember is that people need consistency and stability.

You really need to work at building a sense of stability in new areas. Say you're going into an area and developing one of your sales leaders. One of the worst mistakes you could make is to do only one meeting and think that the area will develop. That is not how things happen. You go out there, you do one meeting and let the people know you're coming back next month. People love that. They're almost surprised and awed that you're really coming back, that you're sincere and that you're going to invest time, effort and energy into their area and their group.

STRUCTURE

Just because we use the word "meeting" does not mean the gathering has to be a formal, highly structured event. Meetings have gone way way beyond the context of what they used to be in the 1960s and 70s. Technology has really allowed for some changes. Meetings can now take place on the telephone—a conference call or a three-way call is a great way to have a meeting. Meetings can take place at get-togethers, socials, dinners, even when you're relaxing at lunch or on the beach in a bathing suit! These meetings don't have to be so highly structured. Yes, you want to have an agenda, you want to have things prepared, you want to cover certain information that will benefit the people/leadership/distributor. But you can be flexible in the way you present your ideas.

PREPARING FOR A MEETING

There are different things you need to prepare for before a meeting. You need to prepare the material you're going talk about at the meeting. You also need to have backup material. I call it plan A, plan B, plan C, plan D, and plan E. I always try to have various options because if something goes wrong, or if I don't get the right feel from the audience, or if I decide I don't want to cover a particular area, or if somebody brings up another topic, I can comfortably leave my plan and go into another area that the people want to talk about. You want to present all the important information that you have prepared, but you also want to work along the lines of people's interests.

MATERIALS NEEDED

A big part of the materials for a meeting is books—books you have on hand or books that people can pick up from you or that they can easily order from someplace. You probably do want to have some books with you so that people can at least start out with the basics.

You also want to be prepared with handouts, flyers, copies of materials and different things you're going to discuss. It doesn't have to be a lot, maybe just one or two pages, but it's something everyone can use to follow along and something they can come away with. You create an atmosphere for the future. Many of my people are scared to death to miss a meeting because I'll give out three or four high-impact handouts and if they're not there, they won't get them. Other materials for the meeting could be audio/visual aids like videos, slides, cassettes and such. I highly recommend that if you're going to be showing or listening to things that it's only for a short time. Don't run a video for thirty minutes unless it's an awesome video that has a lot of power to it.

INVITATIONS

Another key part of preparation is inviting people. By the simple act of inviting you make sure the meeting will be shared with a lot of people and that they will share it with a lot of people and so on. I know a woman who basically built her group by simple invitations. She goes to her local ShopRite food store and is constantly talking to people, whether they are in line to check out or looking at fruit or whatever. She asks them if they have any health challenges or problems and lets them know that there is a meeting they can attend twice a week, Tuesday nights and Thursday mornings, and get answers to any questions they might have about their health. She's been absolutely remarkable in building a group, with from forty to ninety people she's talked to at the grocery store attending at any one time. She shows us all that inviting can be an interesting and a fun part of the business.

SELF-PREPARATION

So you've prepared the material, you've invited the guests, and now you need to prepare your mind. You want your mind to be focused on the meeting. There are always many different things going on in our lives—different things to disrupt and distract us from doing the meeting. What you have to understand, what you have to focus on is the purpose of the meeting. The purpose of the meeting is to give people information on the products. Most products are life-changing. They are going to have a massive impact on your life and the lives of the people that come to the meeting. Remember that you are introducing everyone who attends to an opportunity and an industry that can have a massive impact on their lives. You've got to be able to hurdle over all your personal challenges, things you're involved with, emotions you're experiencing, and you have to focus on the meeting itself. You have to focus on what your mission, your purpose and your goals are.

Once you focus on the purpose, there is something else you can do to prepare mentally. Relax. You're not on trial here, you're not being graded. Some people are going to like the meeting, some people aren't. Some people are going to be excited about it, some people aren't. That's the way it goes.

But even though you're relaxed, you need to be energized and excited about what you're doing. Excitement, passion, enthusiasm, and energy are very, very important. You don't have to necessarily blow the people out the door because you're so excited, but the idea that you're excited about what's going on is important to relate to people. And the more meetings you have, the more relaxed you are about the meetings. Not that you relax the intensity—I'm always excited about the meetings, I always want the meetings to accomplish a lot—but you won't be as stressed and as worried. Everything gets easier with practice. Be confident. If you do your part to prepare, all your meetings will be as successful as you could ever want them to be.

"Me" vs. "We" Mentality

Another important part of preparing a good meeting is to get out of the mentality that meetings are all about "me" and instead turn them into "we" meetings. This is done simply by allowing everyone present to participate in the meeting. The presenter is never the only person to speak. Participation is crucial! Bring everyone into the meeting—their situations, their goals and desires, their challenges, the big events that have happened to them throughout the week. Sharing brings energy and a sense of cohesiveness, and as a result the meeting will become more memorable and more meaningful.

A lot of times I'll have a sales leader or distributor come to the front of the room during a meeting and tell about an herbal hour they've done in the last week. They talk about what happened, how many people came, what kind of products were sold, whether distributors were signed up or not. Most importantly, they give their own personal view of what went on and what kind of growth took place at that particular time. This is awesome because what happens is the people listening get the "me too" concept. They realize that "I can do it too!" This is a part of the "we" mentality. We work with each other and learn from each other and have confidence in each other and our abilities.

Me too!

The purpose of a meeting is not to prove who's the most powerful. It's a time where people can and need to pool their resources and efforts. The #1 situation is where the whole group wins, not just one person. People who want to work and win together look across the line, they see what other people are doing, what other people's visions, dreams and expectations of the industry are. And they try to match those dreams, or make them even better. There need to be a lot of win-win-win-win alliances in this industry. The "we" mentality, the notion of sharing and pooling, is important, especially for people who are starting brand new meetings and building in a new area. It's important that people share ideas right from the get-go so they don't get blown out. There needs to be a free and rapid exchange of information.

WHAT IF WE DON'T HAVE MEETINGS?

Let's turn the tables around. Let's say you've decided you're not going to have meetings. Think of what you have just taken out of the tool box you're building your business with. Basically, you've removed your major power tool. You'll now have to go person to person, doing things in a very unsystematic, laborious manner. If you do not have meetings, you're going to majorly inhibit your future growth. Now when I say future growth, I mean what your growth could be in six or ten years if you *did* do meetings. When you really start to take a look at it, you realize that if you don't do meetings, the likelihood of your downline doing meetings is very remote because no example is being set within your organization. The negative effect, the net loss, is the loss of future growth and future distributors and future sales leaders in your organization. All because you couldn't develop the discipline to overcome the fear that people are judging you, criticizing you, talking about you. Once you get past all that and understand the massive exponential factor that meetings will play in the growth and development of your business, you don't have a choice. You need to do meetings. You need to do meetings and continue to do them well.

CONCLUSION

After reading through this booklet, I hope you begin to realize that it isn't that difficult to have a meeting that everyone enjoys and where something good is accomplished. Meetings educate, empower and increase the vision of each person involved. Those individuals in turn help others to do the same. What happens is that after they hear testimonies about the business and the products, people start to realize that, "Yes! I can do this too! I can feel better, I can achieve better health, I can do the business, I can share this with my friends, I can have a nationwide business, I can succeed." And ideally, that's what we should be getting across in our meetings.

To sum it all up, meetings have massive value. They create momentum, they create a mastermind effect for the group, they keep us on track, get us focused, keep us sharp. At meetings we share opportunities and products. We train people and point them to the tools they need—conference calls, books, pamphlets and other sales aids that will help them do what they need to do. At meetings we learn the thing that motivate us and we work to find out and realize our goals, dreams, and desires. We work on our personal development and focus on being positive so that we get positive results. And once we've learned how to do that, we go and duplicate the process. We have meetings with other people, and they have meetings with other people, etc., on down the line. This sort of sharing is imperative to growth in network marketing. That's what it's all about. And with meetings to empower and focus us, it all becomes possible.